RAYLENE AND SKIP

ALSO BY KENNETH POBO

Books

It Gets Dark So Soon Now (2025)
At the Window, Silence (2025)
Sore Points (2022)
Lilac and Sawdust (2021)
A Preliminary Vision Tested in the Flower (2021)
Uneven Steven (2020)
Wingbuds (2019)
Dindi Expecting Snow (2019)
The Antlantis Hit Parade (2019)
Loplop in a Red City (2017)
Booking Rooms in the Kuiper Belt (2015)
Bend of Quiet (2015)
Glass Garden (2008)
Introductions (2003)
Ordering: A Season in My Garden (2001)
Musings From the Porchlit Sea (1979)

Chapbooks

Hometown Folks (2023)
Gold Bracelet in a Cave: Aunt Stokesia (2022)
Lavender Fire, Lavender Rose (2021)
The Book of Micah (2020)
Your Place or Mine (2020)
Snowflake (2019)
Threads (2019)
Dust and Chrysanthemums (2017)
Calligraphy with Ball (2017)
Highway Rain (2015)
When the Light Turns Green (2014)
Placemats (2013)
Save My Place (2012)
Ice and Gaywings (2011)
Tiny Torn Maps (2011)
Contralto Crows (2011)
Closer Walks (2011)

Tea on Burning Glass (2010)
Fitting Parts (2010)
Trina and the Sky (2009)
Something to Be Said (2009)
Crazy Cakes (2008)
Postcards from America (2004)
Greatest Hits, 1954–2001 (2002)
Open to All (2000)
Cicadas and Apple Trees (1998)
A Barbaric Yawp on the Rocks (1996)
Ravens and Bad Bananas (1995)
Yes: Irises (1992)
Ferns on Fire (1991)
A Pause Inside Dusk (1986)
Evergreen (1985)
Billions of Lit Cigarettes (1981)

RAYLENE AND SKIP

Kenneth Pobo

Wolfson Press
2025

Designed by Sky Santiago.
John Cassels, volume editor.
 First edition.

ISBN: 978-1-950066-20-9

Wolfson Press
Master of Liberal Studies Program
Indiana University South Bend
1700 Mishawaka Avenue
South Bend, Indiana 46634-7111
WolfsonPress.com

For Stan

CONTENTS

ACKNOWLEDGMENTS

Thanks to the editors of the following publications in which poems from this collection first appeared, some in slightly different forms.

Old Northwest Review: "Skip and Raylene and Micah"; "Raylene Imagines Divorcing Skip"
Nthanda Review (Malawi): "Skip and Raylene Share"
London Grip (UK): "Raylene and Skip and Moms"
Cybersoleil: "Strawberries"
Inkwell: "Skip at the Cemetery"
Quiver Review: "Skip and Raylene Simmer"; "Raylene on Her Divorce from Skip"
Silver Stork: "Skip and the Alien"
Sobotka Literary Magazine: "Skip and Raylene"
Nine Cloud Journal: "Skip Bullied"
Illuminations: "Raylene's Hens"
Teach, Write: "Something to Count On"
Comstock Review: "During a Thunderstorm, Raylene" (as "During a Thunderstorm Raylene")
Peculiar: "Bread Instead"
San Pedro River Review: "Raylene and the Vending Machine"
Peeking Cat (UK): "An Accident"; "Long Sleep"
Recasting Masculinity: An Anthology (Beautiful Cadaver Project): "Skip Smoking"
Washington Square Review: "Raylene Tells It" (as "Raylene Tells Me")
Quail Bell Magazine: "Leafwind"
Birdsong Journal: "We Were Happy Once, We Were"
The Great American Wise Ass Anthology (Lamar University Press): "Shucks"
Live Nude Poems: "Raylene Means Well"
The Red Wheelbarrow Review: "During"
Literateur: "Stay Still Moving"; "Skip Revived"
Portland Metrozine: "Loggerheads"
Subtle Tea: "Skip Wants Life"; "Skip Unemployed"
Stratford Quarterly (Canada): "Waiting for It"
Passengers Journal: "Graves, Almost Paid For"

AUTHOR'S NOTE

Though a standalone work, *Raylene and Skip* takes off from a previous collection of mine, *The Book of Micah* (Moonstone Arts Center, 2020), whose poems offer a more fulsome overview of the title characters' Missouri hometown. I often write character poems, and having established Micah broadly as a place, I wanted now to focus on two residents of the town. My interest in creating characters in poetry goes back to my first encounter with the poems of Edwin Arlington Robinson, who populated his Tilbury Town with many wounded and misunderstood people. More recently and specifically, Rita Dove's *Thomas and Beulah*, in which Dove shows us the events and challenges that shape her characters' lives, served as an inspirational template for this book. All of the present poems center on Raylene and/or Skip, but one—"A Flat Sweetness"—breaks the mold somewhat in being delivered by another character, recalling the more multi-vocal *Book of Micah*.

SKIP AND RAYLENE AND MICAH

1. Skip

You want to know what a small town is? It's a bucket
of pig slop I'll kick over on my way out.
I know just about everyone here—more people
hate me close up than anywhere else.
They say I'm a flop, mean, a bad Christian,
I treat Raylene bad. On and on. When I go
I won't leave a forwarding address. I don't
want any hangers-on, even my mother,
her sagging face a condemned church.

2. Raylene

It's true that living here means gossip
is like a thousand mosquitoes let loose
in your house. And there's little chance
to see a Van Gogh exhibit. But
when you wave at someone they generally
wave back. And when I almost died
of meningitis, neighbors brought over food
every night. Would I leave? Yes.
Would I stay? Yes.

SKIP AND RAYLENE SHARE

a love of hens. Every day Raylene
checks for eggs, talks to each one,
has better conversations with them

than with her family, even Skip,
who's normally busy getting ready
for work, but he does ask about

the hens. What's new? They disagree
on a favorite. Raylene says Lydia.
Skip says Barbara.

Raylene says Barbara is very cool—
but Lydia's the brains. What sounds
like clucking is Lydia's chat with

the dead. She says rooster Hank
has a great gig in the salmon-colored
beyond. So does Raylene's mom.

Raylene never hears the dead.
Nor does Skip. Lydia has a way
with eternity, trades feathers for truth.

RAYLENE AND SKIP AND MOMS

On the glider they sip Scotch
and talk about their moms.

Skip resents his: She was a sack
of rules. He squirmed out of it.
Even now seeing her at Christmas

is hard. Raylene says she couldn't
live up to hers, Mary
with the bleeding heart.

Neither talks about their dads,
men like cordoned-off hallways.

It's getting dark. Night,
the one child they have,
soon will be ready to leave.

RAYLENE IMAGINES DIVORCING SKIP

I try to add up all the good,
all the bad, and choose.
Trouble is, I stink at math.
I always get it wrong, so I might
make a bad decision. Bah—

decisions! They make me feel like
life is a bus stop. Either you catch
the bus or you don't and face crap,
like getting fired or your husband
calling you a bitch
as if you missed the bus on purpose.

I'd rather see life as iced tea,
cooling in summer, and in winter
it's still delicious, even the modern kind
that looks like brown powder. Skip
tried to snort it once. Now he
sticks to coffee. Divorce would be

a pleasure, I think, not the loneliness
but the no more explaining myself,
no more raised voices over pork chops.
Who knows? I might

miss him sometimes. I miss
my old suitcase but I
still travel.

STRAWBERRIES

Raylene and Skip argue on the porch
about strawberries.
Are they fresh enough?
They slap each other,
leave marks.

Raylene becomes an ice cube
melting at the bottom of an iced-tea glass,
her grandmother's, with a lilies of the valley pattern.

Skip becomes a saw
sawing the same wood block over and over
until it breaks. The saw clatters
onto the cement basement floor.

The strawberries have no choice
but to overripen, get fuzzy.
Certain they are doomed, they
weep, they scream. Night comes

to the house that opens her doors
to let him in, seduces him.
In the morning a Yellow Cab sun
takes night back home.

SKIP AT THE CEMETERY

Every spring
he drives out to
Ste. Genevieve Memorial Cemetery,
his parents' graves. Hours,

crimson moons
behind chipped stones.

SKIP AND RAYLENE SIMMER

After Skip had the brief affair
with Launa, he thought Raylene
would never find out—here

where gossip outruns rabbits and wind.
Raylene yelled but also didn't care.
Skip was like a bag of groceries,

some good things but some that just
wasted space. They considered
divorcing but Launa moved

to Loyalton. Skip gradually forgot
about her, told Raylene
it shouldn't have happened.

It did happen.
Like in a dream that fades
when you wake up. The plumbing

needs fixing—no one's trustworthy.
Someone will cheat you
the way you cheat others.

SKIP AND THE ALIEN

Skip says that while walking across
the Ritters' cornfield on a Sunday morning
under a blue catcher's-mitt sky, he met

an alien. He liked this being,
not a creature exactly, not human,
nothing as dreary as that. He got
a kindness vibration, something he'd known
little of. Most of life to him
was someone filling his boots with mud,
then making him walk to Dean's Food World.

The alien stood alone—well,
it wasn't standing, more of a spreading,
like a warm June afternoon. For a moment
Skip thought "This alien is God" and that maybe
he should cramp down to his knees and pray,
but he disliked praying, and the alien
didn't seem to require worship. Skip

waved goodbye when the alien
disappeared like a mosquito behind a silo.
Sad, he wondered if they could've been friends,
tossing invisible ropes to planets
all over the galaxy, letting them know
each was loved.

SKIP AND RAYLENE

Raylene says, "You're the type who'd kill me
if I stepped out on you." I smile and drink Jack.
She'd love to turn me into a corpse
that would eventually get her on TV.
I tell her, "I'm on to you. You'll be easy to dispose of."

Here in Micah, people cry
at tribute shows to Neil Diamond
or John Denver.

I don't cry. Ever. When Raylene said she'd be my wife,
I almost cried, but not from happiness.
I saw years of boredom ahead,
as if we were both in a rowboat,
and no matter how hard I tried I could never
get back to shore.

SKIP BULLIED

In first grade, Jim, age 10,
waited for me on my corner
and took my milk money.
I told no one.

Raised Christian, I found
Heaven vague, Hell vivid—
hot, endless. I wish I still
believed in it, Jim screaming
and acting like the Wicked Witch
when Dorothy douses her with water.
I no longer believe that . . .

but . . . what if he's nice now,
a kind man with grandkids
he rocks on creaky knees?

Too late. Hell has gates too,
Mister, and I'm pushing
you through them.

RAYLENE'S HENS

We got chickens on the cheap,
good layers. Aunt Stokesia said
her mother raised Jersey Giants,
played Rudy Vallee
to drown them out. I wearied
of collecting eggs, bosses
who give few vacations.

Chicken shit! Rake it up,
more comes. We sold
the six that survived.
In the grocery store, I walk
quickly past eggs, avoid
chicken pieces under
clear wrappings. Even cake mixes
disturb. They're probably

dead by now. The long summer
light coaxing them to lay,
apron pockets full
of perfect spheres,
breakable beauty.

SOMETHING TO COUNT ON

Skip spent almost $4,000
on a custom-made gun.
Raylene barely spoke to him
for a week. He shrugged.
With Skip, you pound
a shrug's red brick wall—
no way to tear it down.

He has few friends
but many buddies
who like Cal's Tap
and sports and laughing
at wives, girlfriends,
or, if they have no one,
to blame women. A good friend,

Skip holds the gun
with tenderness, only
uses it on special hunts.
It stays in the basement
under lock and the key
to his heart.

DURING A THUNDERSTORM, RAYLENE

leaves the La-Z-Boy and walks out
to the ladder leaning against
the house to get to the slanted roof,
dangerous even on a dry day—

she stands above her house
and calls down gods and goddesses
of lightning. Angels may come too.
Skip charges outside, yells at her,
and demands that she come down.
To her, he looks small and wet,
a tiny cat near the boxwood bush.
Lightning jackknifes the sky. She
raises her arms, laughs. Skip climbs
up to get her, she backs away.

When the storm weakens, she
comes in, takes a hot shower.
It's like she never left. Skip
reads the *Micah Times*. Not many times
in Micah, just one day carving up
another, a bar beer, work.

Raylene cooks weenies and baked beans.
Burps and a *Hee Haw* rerun.

BREAD INSTEAD

Skip says, "Bake something for my mom."
He drives off to deliver propane,
tunes in oldies radio, songs that make him

13 again, needing comfort
after his dad said "Goodbye Sport"
for good. Mom worked at Lane's Bakery,
gone by 4:00 AM each weekday. Skip
means to stay in better touch,
sprawls on the couch. Raylene
bristles when told to cook,
imagines hollowing out
Skip's head, using it as a vase

for glads. She bakes bread instead,
not for his mother, mostly for herself,
the way she likes it, heavy
on the flour so it gets hard,
butter scrambling over each crumb.

The kitchen smells like her Nana's did
two decades ago, warm,
before the eviction.

RAYLENE AND THE VENDING MACHINE

I may be a good-hearted woman,
but don't mistake me
for a doormat. Skip goes out,

tries to have a good time,
and expects me to understand.
Even when he's home,

he's buried in a game
like Super Mario Bros.
or Duck Hunt.

Would I laugh or cry if
I saw his chair catch fire
with him in it?

Love is like a vending machine.
You can get some sweet things,
not too good for you. You want

more, something substantial.
And you've already run out
of quarters.

AN ACCIDENT

Raylene met Skip in high school,
thought he was cool, despite a rumor
that he'd killed his cousin Lena. Oh well,
surely it was an accident. He wouldn't turn

violent, would he? They married
when she was 20, he 21. It's been crummy,
she thinks, but fears
it's probably worse alone—

like her Aunt Flynn who sees the Virgin
in her mashed potatoes and prays
to meet someone as she spoons on gravy.

PAPER CUP

For most of high school, Raylene
ate lunch alone, came home
to reruns of *Green Acres*.

High school was
the garbage truck. It stank—
but it did pass by.

After graduation, she watched
four years float like a paper cup
down Crane Creek.

SKIP SMOKING

A voyeur moon
at the window. He looks
at her increasing years
as a punching bag,
gives a hard left hook,
can't knock them down.

He's 34 cigarettes,
all burning at once.

RAYLENE TELLS IT

The neighbor's son died of
fentanyl.
Just out of high school.
His family held a prayer vigil,
believes in miracles.

Closed stores, merchants
can't make it. Wal-Mart
drove out three grocery stores.
The gun shop open,
army supply store too.
Dusk on

a cornfield, it's still
beautiful here.

The young leave,
sometimes in caskets.

LEAFWIND

Skip drives as if the road
springs out from his glove compartment—
  fast
is how he gets through life.

His grandmother nags him to stop
and smell the roses. Stop?
Why not just roll up miles,
make them small as a pill
to pop? Raylene
hoped that marriage
would change him—she finds
his glove compartment cramped.

As a kid he felt rootless,
a wind-caught leaf, learned to press
the pedal, keep one step ahead
of any breeze. Now he knows
no other way to be. Someday,
he thinks, he's going
  to crash—

it won't be a bad accident,
it will be deliberate,
the leaf plucked in midair,
speed like a priest
providing last rites.

WE WERE HAPPY ONCE, WE WERE

My grandmother said Skip
would hurt me. Uncle Dave,
a closed garage door at the wedding,
no expression. My parents said
congratulations, seemed happy,
but they often seemed happy.

We started out well,
like the year's first crocus,
lavender in March sun. Then
a short, stormy spring—
I had guessed we'd be stormy.
We're both stormy.

We look out a window at
unyielding gray,
held in its grip.

SHUCKS

Raylene says, "You're the type who'd forgive me
if I stepped out on you." I say shucks and tell her I love her
even more than our dog Wizard. She cries
wet atomic warheads. They explode
on our anniversaries. Or in messy weather.

I prefer fishing and tell Raylene, "Baby, I'll miss you so bad."
She puts her arms around me, squeezes my ass,
waves as my pickup peels out for the Delmarva.

Speaking of pickups, that's the real reason
I head to eastern Maryland—to pick up
women, if I can get them.

One got nasty and I shot her in the face.
She never told. In fact, she asked to see me again.
I said no. I was married. She understood.

I tell Raylene when I get home how nothing was biting.
She heats up those Gorton fish sticks
that we eat with *Family Feud*,
a good lead-in to sex. Sometimes
that gets kind of nuclear. Afterwards,

we feel vaporized, gone yet fully present.

RAYLENE MEANS WELL

Her pillow is
ringing bells.
She can't sleep.
Several cathedrals
pound in her ears.
It must mean
something,
a new beginning,
a truth that breaks
out, sets a fire.

DURING

the power outage they make
love, something to do

when Raylene would normally be
watching *The Price Is Right*,
Skip looking for fast cars
or girls online.

Snow insults
the picture window.
Icicles crab down gutters.

Afterwards, on a wool
comforter, they watch a TV
that stays utterly blank.

STAY STILL MOVING

In Micah, barns float
like air balloons. Cows
teach pebbles how to moo.
The town has a light
that turns heads
into kaleidoscopes. Turn
one way and color's magic. Turn
another and colors clash. Or

try to stay still,
a sagging porch
barely holding up
a wringer washer
and rusty swing.

GO, STAY

When Raylene caught Skip
flirting with Alicia Conway,
who flirts back, she pushed hard
against his Adam's apple—
Skip collapsed,
got up and washed the car.
Their anniversary, cake and cuts.
    I can't go.
    I can't stay.

Years wag by the kitchen door,
want to get out. No one opens it.
Even the house would scurry off
its foundations, but it needs paint
and to be lived in.

A FLAT SWEETNESS

Ask him his favorite color.
He says blue. I'm his best friend—
I know better. He says a blue sky
is like a busted vein, prefers yellow
but keeps that a secret. A man

of many secrets. Raylene found out
about Juanita the waitress.
He said she was just helping him
with his popcorn popper. She could
fix anything. Raylene shrugs off his lies.
When he says, "Ray, I love you," she knows
he means himself. She calls him
a snowball melting on a window sill.
The sun burns away all his lies,

leaves nothing. Skip says, "I had a fight
with truth. It happened in first grade.
I told the truth, that I had stolen
a dime from my teacher Mrs. Wright.
I got expelled *and* a whippin'."

He walked away from truth.
It wasn't reliable. Coke—
until the fizz falls away and only
a flat sweetness remains.

LONG SLEEP

Raylene believes that all of her cats
will go to Heaven. Skip says no,

they just go and that's that. She
says cockroaches don't go to Heaven—
why would God want them crawling up
gold streets, living in tidy mansions?
Skip says cockroaches might get
a better place than most people—
who are mean, lazy, arrogant.
Raylene says that Skip is mean,
lazy, arrogant. He says yes,
but I don't care about Heaven—
it sounds like a kid's game
where only the athletes get picked.

Raylene holds their cat Huzzah
and says he will be going to Heaven
even if Skip won't be there. Huzzah
cries to eat. Fed, he takes a long sleep,
heaven in a mamasan chair.

SKIP REVIVED

I collapse
and doctors bring me back
in a hospital. Mom asks
what did I see?
Nothing, I saw nothing—

the roof turns
weathered shingles to the sun
and exhales.

LOGGERHEADS

Raylene sees her mother as a parking meter taking quarters but providing no time. They fight and don't talk for days. Her mother watches sitcoms because by 8:25 everyone hugs. Raylene prefers detective shows, the crime like a joke, and she tries to guess the punchline.

She wishes she and her mother could share a sniff of a Tropicana rose by the back door. The bush won't survive a bad winter.

SKIP WANTS LIFE

to be fun as a county fair
tractor pull, big equipment
facing off. Someone wins,
not like in schools where
no one can lose. His folks

call him a loser,
even Raylene does.
She sighs for Charley Benthorp—
he's a winner, runs a gun shop
outside Kansas City.

It's the world's fault.
It's life's fault.

Tractors grunt and groan,
their version of public sex.
Once again, Dorgan wins,
his farm on the edge
of bankruptcy—the blue ribbon
on the red tractor
with rusting wheels.

RAYLENE ON HER DIVORCE FROM SKIP

before we did it, maybe
it was good or good enough or terrible
with good moments, a kaleidoscope,

colors changing constantly, I wished
just for even a day they'd stay the same,
but they change I change

he changes and sometimes
I imagined cutting his dick off
but then I thought now why would I

want to hurt him since sometimes
loving him is bolt-upright nice until
colors start changing again so much so

that my eyes ache and if the Goodwill
people came by and offered
a whole quarter for my heart

I'd grab the money, buy a gumball,
and blow bubbles as anonymous
cars pass the sold house

SKIP UNEMPLOYED

Another job gone. I worked in Al's Pawn Shop
for a year, a FOR SALE on the door.
I doubt anyone will bite.

Why bite here? I'd rather be a perch
washed up on a shore than live here.
Jackson Street used to thrive. Purple Martin
houses up by the courthouse fell. Even
birds go elsewhere. I used to work

on a farm. I'm good with my hands—except
when they touch people. I mostly ruin
whoever I touch. I grab too hard. I just
want to feel something real, cage
breath like a firefly in a jar. Give me

a backhoe and I'll fix it, but the farm went
the same direction as Ruby's Diner,
a FOR SALE there too. I've heard
it may be demolished
in the heart of a town that's turning
into an empty space.

WAITING FOR IT

Darkness skins its knees—
suddenly there's morning.
The sun prods with gold pitchforks.

Raylene walks out into the light
waiting for a revelation, a bus
scheduled to arrive
but it never does. A black butterfly,
blue on the bottom of both wings,
grabs a sunflower.
This is the moment!

It flies away. A cloud rolls up
torn sleeves and glowers.

GRAVES, ALMOST PAID FOR

Last year Raylene and Skip
bought graves,

one pine tree to shade both.
Even in death there's no sep-

aration. Eventually
no one will visit—

dandelions yellowing
an impressive silence.

About the Author

Kenneth Pobo (he/him) grew up in Illinois and now lives in Pennsylvania with his husband and cat. He began writing at the age of 15, inspired by songs like "Crystal Blue Persuasion" by Tommy James and the Shondells, and his Midwestern roots have continued to influence his writing. For 33 years he taught English and creative writing at Widener University in Chester, Pennsylvania. In 2020 he retired from teaching—but not from writing. He focuses mostly on poetry and flash fiction, with many of his poems being character studies and including garden-centered imagery. He also enjoys writing ekphrastic poems exploring connections with other forms of art, often painting or music. He is the author of 33 chapbooks and seventeen full-length collections. Recent books include *Bend of Quiet* (Blue Light Press), *Loplop in a Red City* (Circling Rivers), *Sore Points* (Finishing Line Press), *Lilac and Sawdust* (Meadowlark Press), *Lavender Fire, Lavender Rose* (BrickHouse Books), *Gold Bracelet in a Cave: Aunt Stokesia* (Ethel Press), and recently from Fernwood Press, a book of poems called *At the Window, Silence,* and from Broken Tribe, *It Gets Dark So Soon Now*. His work has appeared in *North Dakota Quarterly, Amsterdam Review, Asheville Poetry Review, Nimrod, Indiana Review, Mudfish, Hawaii Review, Southern Indiana Review*, and elsewhere.